EMMITT SMITH

NFL Super Runner

BY BILL GUTMAN

MILLBROOK SPORTS WORLD
THE MILLBROOK PRESS
BROOKFIELD, CONNECTICUT

Photographs courtesy of Allsport: cover (Jonathan Daniel),
cover inset (Mike Powell), pp. 20–21 (Allen Dean Steele), 37
(Bill Hickey), 44 (Bill Hickey), 46 (Otto Greule); Wide World:
pp. 3, 28, 35; NFL Photos: pp. 4 (James D. Smith), 25 (Scott
Cunningham), 27 (James D. Smith), 31 (George Rose), 34 (Peter
Read Miller), 43 (Peter Read Miller); Gary McCracken: pp. 9,
11, 12, 14, 19; University of Florida: p. 17; Vern Biever: pp.
32–33; Louis DeLuca, *The Dallas Morning News:* pp. 40–41.

Library of Congress Cataloging-in-Publication Data
Gutman, Bill.
Emmitt Smith, NFL super runner / by Bill Gutman.
p. cm. — (Millbrook sports world)
Includes bibliographical references and index.
Summary: A biography of football running back Emmitt Smith,
from his childhood to his early success at the University of Florida
to his stardom as 1994 Super Bowl MVP for the Dallas Cowboys.
ISBN 1-56294-501-7
1. Smith, Emmitt—Juvenile literature. 2. Football players—
United States—Biography—Juvenile literature. 3. Running
backs (Football)—United States—Biography—Juvenile literature.
4. National Football League—Juvenile literature. [1. Smith,
Emmitt. 2. Football players. 3. Afro-Americans—Biography.]
I. Title. II. Series.
GV939.S635G88 1995
796.332′092—dc20 [B] 94-21836 CIP AC

Published by The Millbrook Press
2 Old New Milford Road
Brookfield, Connecticut 06804

EMMITT SMITH

It was a rainy late October afternoon in Philadelphia. The artificial turf at Veterans Stadium was wet and slippery. The Philadelphia Eagles were playing host to the Dallas Cowboys in the seventh game of the 1993 National Football League season. Both teams came in with 4–2 records. So it was a big game for each.

Dallas had a fine young quarterback in Troy Aikman and an All-Pro wide receiver in Michael Irvin. But on this wet October afternoon, the passing game wasn't working. In fact, the Dallas offense might have stalled if it wasn't for the play of the team's outstanding running back.

Emmitt Smith set the tone on the Cowboys' first drive. The team marched 81 yards before kicking a field goal. Emmitt gained 55 of those yards with darting, slashing runs. At the end of the first quarter Dallas had a 3–0 lead and Smith had already gained 65 yards. He ran for 64 more in the second period as Dallas took a 10–7 lead at the half. Emmitt had now gained 129 yards. Most backs don't gain that much in an entire game.

Emmitt Smith proved his power in the seventh game of the 1993 season. Playing on a wet field in Philadelphia, the star running back of the Dallas Cowboys carried the ball thirty times, cutting and slashing his way to a 237-yard day. The Cowboys won, 23–10.

The third period was a defensive battle. The teams swapped field goals as Emmitt ran for only 14 yards. Dallas held a 13–10 lead going into the final quarter as the rain fell harder. But everyone knew that either team could still win.

Then in the fourth period, Emmitt Smith really took over. With many of the other players slipping and sliding on the soaked turf, Emmitt kept gaining yards. He was running hard, churning and cutting on the wet field. With 3:45 left in the game, Dallas had a 16–10 lead and had the ball on its own 38-yard line. Once again, quarterback Aikman took the snap and gave the ball to Emmitt.

The 5-foot-9 (175-centimeter), 210-pound (95-kilogram) running back burst right up the middle. A couple of Eagles defenders grabbed at him, but his powerful legs allowed him to run right though them. He made a quick cut and was past the safety. Emmitt won the footrace to the end zone, completing a 62-yard touchdown run to put the game out of reach.

When it ended, the Cowboys had a 23–10 victory and Emmitt Smith had set a team record by gaining 237 yards on 30 carries. It was an incredible performance under terrible conditions by a runner who had led the NFL with 1,713 yards gained in 1992.

"Smith's run broke our backs," said Philadelphia coach Rich Kotite after the game.

"Emmitt is a great back and had great footing," Cowboys coach Jimmy Johnson added. "He has a low base and it's hard to get under him. He was able to circle and spin all afternoon."

Not bad for a player who some NFL scouts thought was too small and too slow to be a pro star. But Emmitt Smith had been finding ways to gain yardage on a football field since he was a small boy. He was a superstar in high school, an All-American in college, and an All-Pro in the National Football League. Now, more and more people were calling him one of the best of all time.

FOOTBALL AND FAMILY

There are two words that best describe Emmitt Smith; they are *football* and *family*. These are the two things that have been most important in his life. He has never been caught up in the hype of being a football star. He takes care of business on the gridiron. Then comes his family. Other things have to wait.

Emmitt James Smith III was born on May 15, 1969, in Pensacola, Florida. That's where his family still lives, and it's the place he calls home. He was the second child born to Mary and Emmitt Smith, Jr. His sister Marsha was the oldest. After Emmitt came Erik, Emory, Emil, and Connie.

Since Emmitt had the same name as his father and grandfather, his mother gave him a nickname immediately. She called him "Scoey," after her favorite comedian, Scoey Mitchell. Although he has remained "Scoey" to his family, the football world has always known him as Emmitt.

The Smiths were a hardworking family. His grandfather did heavy labor on the night shift at the Armstrong Industries plant in Pensacola. He never missed a day's work in the 40 years before his retirement in 1986. His father, Emmitt, Jr., worked at a bus depot and often drove the buses. His mother, Mary, waited until her children were in school, then became a document clerk at a Pensacola bank.

As soon as they could afford it, Emmitt's parents built a house right next to his grandparents' house on North G Street. Emmitt often spent the nights with his grandmother. His grandfather was working, and his grandmother, Irma Lee, was an invalid.

Emmitt used to sit and talk with her for hours at a time. He would bring her food and later lift her from her wheelchair and put her in bed.

"We're a family and we do things for each other," his grandfather said. "Even when he was just 12 or 13 years old, he was always here when he was supposed to be. That boy has always brought joy to this house. He's been a blessing."

Today, a large poster of Emmitt hangs on the living room wall in his grandparents' house. On it Emmitt wrote: "To Grandma. Thanks for life and your love and your support."

Emmitt's mother often invited other neighborhood children in and gave them hot meals. But she wouldn't put up with any fighting or teasing, foul language, smoking, or drugs.

An old family friend, Marzette Porterfield, who met Emmitt in the sixth grade, said that many of the neighborhood youngsters were a little jealous of Emmitt.

"It wasn't because of what he could do on the football field," she said. "It was the house and his family. They were special, and he got to live there with them."

Football found a place alongside family very early. When Emmitt was still a baby, his mother would often put him in a swing in front of the television. She would give him a bottle, then find a football game for him to watch.

"It was about the only way to keep him quiet then," she recalled.

As soon as he was old enough to play, Emmitt looked for games of

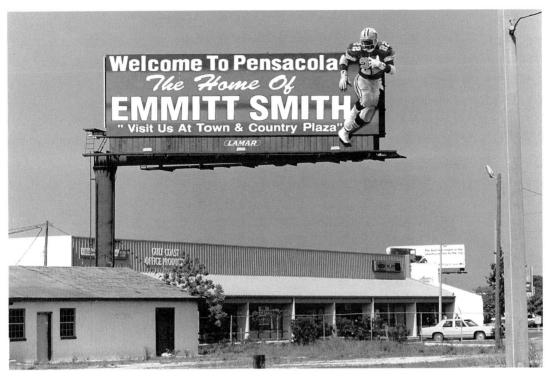

Emmitt has remained faithful to his hometown of Pensacola, Florida, and has never wanted to live anywhere else. As this sign shows, Pensacola is proud of Emmitt, too.

tackle, not touch. His didn't want his mother to worry about him, so he would turn his clothes inside out when he played. That way, when he turned them right side out again, the dirt and grass from rough games wouldn't show.

When Emmitt was 7 he began playing in a league for the first time. Even then he was broad in the shoulders and heavy in the thighs. His opponents found him very hard to bring down. By the time he was 8 he was so good that he was put in a league with 10-year-olds. And when he was 11 he began playing against 14-year-olds. He was already a muscular 145 pounds (66 kilograms), too good and too strong for the kids his age. There even were times when he had to lose weight to play in the youth league games.

At the age of 12 he led his team to a big victory against a team from Mobile, Alabama. The 16-year-olds on the Mobile team simply couldn't find a way to stop Emmitt Smith.

By the time Emmitt reached Escambia High School in Pensacola in the fall of 1983 he was already 5 feet 8 (173 centimeters) and 175 pounds (79 kilograms). He was just 14 years old and ready to dazzle everyone with his football talent. But he still looked back to his family as a source of strength. He explained his feelings years later. "There is nothing that I am today that I would be without family," was the way he put it. "I inherited my athletic skills, and I learned all about life—how to love, how to act, how to treat people, how to expect to be treated—from my family. It's family, not football, that has been the greatest gift of all. I could get hurt tomorrow, and football would be over. Family will always be there."

HIGH SCHOOL ALL-AMERICAN

Football is a huge sport in the Florida Panhandle area. There are many outstanding players who hope to get college scholarships. The games are usually hard fought. Competition is fierce. It was no different when Emmitt played. He was just a 14-year-old freshman, but his coach, Dwight Thomas, had high hopes for him.

"Kid," he said, "I want you to gain 5 miles for me."

What Coach Thomas meant was that he planned to use Emmitt as his number one running back right from the opening game of the 1983 season. Emmitt didn't disappoint him. In his first high school game he ran for 115 yards against Pensacola Catholic High. The Emmitt Smith era had begun.

Before his freshman year ended, Emmitt had games of 205, 183, 189, and 210 yards. He failed to reach 100 yards only twice. He finished with an amazing total of 1,525 yards. And he was just warming up.

In 1984 he was already the most feared running back in his district. Many defensive units would tape his number, 24, on their helmets, to remind each other of the player they had to stop. But no one could stop Emmitt. Running with a low center of gravity and that short, powerful stride, he kept piling up the yards and scoring touchdowns.

At Escambia High School, Emmitt was a star running back right from his freshman year.

In high school, Emmitt was an unselfish player who didn't mind letting others play once the game was well in hand.

Although Emmitt never bragged about his skills or showed off on the field, he set high goals for himself and was confident he could reach them.

"Ever since high school, when I became aware of what 1,000 yards seemed to mean to people, I began to set goals for myself," Emmitt said. "My first was 1,500 yards a season, and I made it every year in high school."

The numbers continued to mount. In his sophomore year he completed games of 236, 227, 218, 215, and 200 yards. Once again he failed to reach 100 yards only twice. He finished the season with an incredible 2,424 yards in 14 games as Escambia won the state championship.

Even more amazing was the fact that he ran for so many yards while often playing half a game or less.

"My theory was to play a lot of kids," said Coach Thomas, "and as soon as a game was in hand, we pulled the first string. In some games, Emmitt carried fewer than ten times. But he was always an unselfish player, a special player who never complained about anything."

By his junior year it was apparent that Emmitt was becoming one of the top high school running backs in the country. He had seven games in which he gained more than 200 yards.

One game, against Milton High, was a close one in which Emmitt had to stay in all the way. It was 21–21 at the end of regulation and went into overtime. Escambia finally won it, 24–21, with Emmitt running for 301 yards on 28 carries. That's an average of 10.75 yards a try.

At one point in the season he ran for more than 200 yards in five straight games. When it ended Escambia had another state title, and Emmitt had run for 2,918 yards in 14 games, or an average of 208 yards per game. Not surprisingly, Emmitt was named to a number of high school All-American teams after the season.

Many college recruiters were beginning to seek out the Smiths to speak with Emmitt and his family. But Mary Smith set down some strict rules. The recruiters were allowed to speak with Emmitt only on Sundays. Between school, football, and taking care of his grandmother at night, Emmitt had a full schedule. And, in truth, he really wasn't interested in most of the schools that wanted him.

"I didn't want my family to have to go all over the country to see me play," Emmitt said. "I wanted to stay close to home."

During his senior season, Emmitt signed a letter of intent to attend the University of Florida at nearby Gainesville. On the day he signed, he arrived with a number of his lesser-known Escambia teammates.

Although many colleges wanted him, Emmitt decided to
stay close to home. As his mother sits beside him, Emmitt
announces that he will attend the University of Florida.

"I thought it would be nice to spread the limelight around," Emmitt said. "I wanted to give some guys a day to remember."

By this time, there was little doubt about Emmitt's talent. The Escambia team had lost a number of top players the year before and wasn't as good overall. In 1986, they didn't even go to the state playoffs, but Emmitt still gained 1,937 yards in 11 games. He was a consensus High School All-American and named Player of the Year by several local organizations.

His numbers were mind-boggling. In four years he gained 8,804 yards (a total of 5 miles, or 8 kilometers) on 1,127 carries, an average of 7.8 yards a carry. He scored 107 touchdowns, 106 on the ground, and fumbled the ball only six times. He had run for more than 100 yards in 45 of his 49 high school games. He was over the 200-yard mark 17 times and cracked the 300-yard barrier once.

When his high school career ended, his coach made no secret of what Emmitt had meant to the team.

"For four years we did three things and won two state championships doing them," Dwight Thomas said. "They were hand the ball to Emmitt, pitch the ball to Emmitt, and throw the ball to Emmitt. It was no secret. Everyone knew we were going to get the ball to him. It was just a question of how."

Before leaving Escambia, Emmitt represented the nation's high school football players at President Ronald Reagan's "Say No to Drugs" campaign in Washington, D.C. In fact, whenever someone would ask Emmitt how he avoided getting involved with drugs or teenage gangs, he would give them a strange look and say, "It just never occurred to me."

FRESHMAN SENSATION

There was little doubt about the kind of person who was going to the University of Florida in the fall of 1987. But there were still some who doubted his ability. Emmitt was now 5 feet 9 (175 centimeters) and a solid 190 pounds (86 kilograms). Some critics said he was too slow and didn't have the quickness or cutting ability to be a big-time college runner.

It was true that Emmitt didn't have blazing speed or a variety of fancy "moves." But it's impossible to measure a man's instinct for the game or the size of his heart. It didn't take Emmitt long to prove his critics completely wrong.

He came off the bench in the first couple of games of the year. But when he gained 109 yards against Tulsa, Coach Galen Hall decided he would give his freshman a start against powerful Alabama. The result was a "first start" matched by few collegiate runners.

With the game on national television, Emmitt carried the ball 39 times. That was a school record in itself. So was the 224 yards he gained while scoring a pair of touchdowns and showing the entire country that there was a new star running back ready to make his mark. Florida won the game, 23–14.

In the next three weeks Emmitt ran for 173, 184, and 130 yards. And when he gained 175 yards in a 34–3 victory against Temple in the seventh game of the season, he cracked the 1,000-yard mark faster than any other player in college football history. He was a national record-setter already.

But he still wasn't finished. Emmitt was a model of consistency all year. He ran for an even 100 yards in a 28–14 loss against powerful rival Florida State. And he finished the year with a 128-yard game as the Gators lost to UCLA in the Aloha Bowl, 20–16.

It had truly been a freshman year to remember. The team's record was just 6–6, but Emmitt wound up with 1,341 yards on 229 carries, an

With his great balance and great vision, Emmitt became a star as soon as he began playing for the Gators.

average of 5.9 yards a pop. He also caught 25 passes for another 184 yards and scored 13 touchdowns on the ground. His rushing yards were the best in the Southeastern Conference (SEC) and good for tenth place among the nation's runners.

Even as his fame grew, he continued to show respect for his family. During one home game in Gainesville that his parents attended, Emmitt did a dance in the end zone after scoring a touchdown. It was a hotdog move that many players in college and the pros perform. But Emmitt's father didn't like it. After the game he simply said to his son, "We'll have no more of that."

Emmitt never did a dance again. After that, whenever he scored a touchdown he simply laid the ball down and trotted off the field.

GATOR SUPERSTAR

In Emmitt's sophomore year of 1988 the numbers continued to mount. Against Montana State he had 148 yards and ran for three touchdowns as the Gators romped, 69–0. In a 17–0 victory over Mississippi State he had 164 yards on just 13 carries. He scored twice, once on a 96-yard run, the longest in team history. No one was saying he was slow now.

He reached the 2,000-yard mark for his Florida career in the fifth game. Only Herschel Walker had reached that milestone faster, having done it in the third game of his sophomore year. Emmitt was tied for second with another running legend, Tony Dorsett.

Though he didn't quite match the season he had as a freshman, Emmitt still managed 988 yards on 187 carries in 1988. That was good for a

5.3 per carry average, and he scored nine touchdowns. He capped off the season with a sensational 159-yard performance, as Florida topped Illinois in the All-America Bowl, 14–10, to finish their season at 7–5.

There was little doubt about Emmitt's ability now, but he still felt he could do better. During the summer he returned home, where once again he helped to care for his grandmother, spent time with his family, worked out to stay in shape, and tried to make up for lost time with his studies. He was a therapeutic recreation major at Florida and always tried hard to keep his grades up. He was determined to graduate.

But when he returned to Florida for his junior year of 1989, there were some storm clouds on the horizon. The Gators were being investigated by the National Collegiate Athletic Association (NCAA) for not following NCAA rules on recruiting athletes. Sometimes the NCAA punishes schools that break the rules by

By the fifth game of his sophomore year, Emmitt had already gained more than 2,000 yards. Although he never claimed to have blazing speed, in the open field he was tough to catch and even tougher to bring down.

Emmitt started his junior year of 1989 with a 117-yard game against Mississippi. Here he sheds the Ole Miss line for a solid gain, leaving tacklers in his wake.

taking away some scholarships. Or it might not allow the team to play on national television or go to a bowl game.

These possibilities made the season difficult on the players. But Emmitt somehow managed to focus on his game all year long. He was a star nearly every week. Once again he began to pile up the yardage. Against Mississippi State he had 182 yards, his best game in the early going, as the Gators won, 21–0. Then, at midseason, he put together two of the greatest games in SEC history.

The first was in a 34–11 win over Vanderbilt. Emmitt ran the ball 25 times for 202 yards, an average of 8.1 yards per carry. He was Co-SEC Player of the Week for that one. What happened the following week was even more amazing. The Gators were going to meet New Mexico on Saturday. Then, during the week, Coach Galen Hall resigned suddenly, and the team's starting quarterback was kicked off the team.

With all that happening, many people felt that the Gators would be beaten. That was before Emmitt Smith began running wild. Emmitt proved nearly unstoppable, ripping off one big gain after another. When the smoke cleared, the Gators had a 27–21 victory and Emmitt Smith had gained 316 yards on 31 carries, scoring three touchdowns along the way.

In that one game alone, Emmitt had broken 15 school records. He was named Offensive Player of the Week by several national organizations. And he also had passed Neal Anderson as Florida's all-time leading rusher to become the first Gator back to run for 200 or more yards in two straight games. One newspaper story said what many people were thinking: "If there's a better collegiate running back than Emmitt Smith, we'd like to see him."

That was hard to dispute. Emmitt finished his junior year on a strong note, gaining 153 yards on 30 carries in the Gators' final game, a 24–17 loss to powerful Florida State. But what a year it had been! Emmitt's final numbers were 1,599 yards on 284 carries, a 5.6 per carry average, and 14 touchdowns. He caught another 21 passes for 207 yards and one more score.

Needless to say, he was a consensus All-American and finished seventh in the voting for the Heisman Trophy, an award given to the player considered the best in the land. His average of 145.4 rushing yards per game was third best in the nation. Amazingly, he fumbled the ball just once all year. After three years he had 3,928 yards on 700 carries for a 5.6 average. He had already set an amazing 58 school records. With another year remaining, he would have to be considered one of the favorites to win the Heisman.

A SURPRISE DECISION

There was a major change in the National Football League draft rules prior to the 1990 season. For the first time ever, college juniors would be allowed to pass up their final year of college play and enter the NFL. That spring, Emmitt spent hours on the telephone talking to his family back home in Pensacola. He had a big decision to make.

Should he stay at Florida for his senior year, or should he enter the NFL draft and become a professional? Florida was still being investigated by the NCAA. The football program at the university was in turmoil. The coach had resigned, and several players had left the team. The upcoming season held little promise.

Emmitt was already known as one of the best running backs in the land. He had nothing left to prove as a collegiate runner. Finally, he notified the NFL to put his name in the upcoming draft. He would leave Florida and turn pro.

Now the question was, where would Emmitt play? Most felt he would be a high draft pick. But there were those who still said he was too slow. He didn't have the blinding speed most superstar runners have. One who felt that didn't matter was Joe Brodsky, the backfield coach of the Dallas Cowboys.

"I worked Emmitt out at Gainesville," said Brodsky. "You'd have to be an idiot not to recognize his talent. He was a guy who would play in pain, never missed a workout, wasn't a nick-and-bump guy who'd miss a lot of practice. He was an extra-good worker and not a complainer."

That was good enough for Cowboys coach Jimmy Johnson. He had seen Emmitt play at Florida because he had coached the nearby University of Miami. Johnson held his breath until it was Dallas's time to choose. The Cowboys had the 17th pick in the first round and promptly took Emmitt. He was the second running back chosen.

Emmitt would be joining a team that was rebuilding. The Cowboys had been a great NFL franchise since they joined the league in 1960. Under Coach Tom Landry, they had won a host of division titles and had been to the Super Bowl five times. But in the mid-1980s the team faltered. In 1989 a businessman named Jerry Jones bought the Cowboys. Jones hired Jimmy Johnson as the new coach.

With many new players, the Cowboys had struggled to a dismal 1–15 record in 1989. But they had a fine young quarterback in Troy Aikman, and now they had drafted Emmitt Smith. It took almost the entire preseason for Emmitt and the Cowboys to agree on the contract. Then, shortly before the opening game, he signed a three-year deal for $2.2 million. He was finally ready to play.

Emmitt wasn't a starter in the first game of the season, because he needed more time to learn the Dallas plays. He carried the ball just twice and gained only 2 yards. A week later he was in the starting lineup, but gained only 11 yards on six carries.

Then three weeks later against Tampa Bay, Emmitt began to really show his stuff. He carried the ball 23 times for 121 yards. It was his first 100-yard game in the NFL. He would have two more 100-yard games before the year ended. The Cowboys improved to 7–9 in 1990, and Emmitt finished the year with 937 yards on 241 carries, an average of 3.9 yards a try. He also scored 11 touchdowns.

When the season was over, the Associated Press named him NFL Offensive Rookie of the Year, and he was named on all the All-Rookie teams. His rushing total was the best among rookie running backs, and he finished tenth in rushing in the NFL.

By this time, Emmitt weighed nearly 210 pounds (95 kilograms) and was very strong with a low center of gravity. He had great leg drive and was described by a Cowboys coach as being "quick within a confined space." Defensive players never seemed to get a solid hit on him. That was why he was rarely hurt.

As for Emmitt, he enjoyed the idea that so many people could not really describe his running style. "I'm an enigma," he said, "an unknown. You can't really figure out what I'm going to do next. I like it like that."

Early in his rookie year with the Cowboys, Emmitt showed the Washington Redskins that he would be a tough running back to control.

ALL-PRO RUSHING CHAMP

In 1991 both the Cowboys and Emmitt Smith came of age. Coach Johnson had rebuilt the team quickly. There were many fine young players who were getting better. Quarterback Aikman was quickly becoming one of the best passers in the league. Wide receiver Michael Irvin was also among the best at his position. And Emmitt Smith was about to show everyone that he was a runner to be feared.

Emmitt opened the season with two straight 112-yard games. In the second game against Washington, he broke loose for a 75-yard touchdown run. That silenced some of the critics who said he was too slow. Two games later he showed superstar talent to everyone. In a Dallas win over Phoenix, Emmitt bulled, twisted, faked, and sprinted his way to a 182-yard game, carrying the ball 23 times and breaking away for a touchdown run of 60 yards.

After that, every defense had to key on Emmitt. Because they feared Emmitt's running, Aikman's passing became even more effective. It was the kind of pass-run balance that all teams try to have. Later in the season he had three straight 100-yard-plus games and finished the regular schedule with a 160-yard effort against Atlanta.

Two years after finishing at 1–15, the Cowboys had improved to 11–5 and were back in the playoffs. With Quarterback Aikman hurt late in the season, more of the pressure fell on Emmitt. He had delivered with four 100-yard games in his last five. That gave him an NFL best of 1,563 yards on 365 carries for the season. He averaged 4.3 yards a try and scored 12 touchdowns. He also caught 49 passes for another 258 yards. It was an All-Pro performance.

In the wild-card playoff game, Dallas topped the Chicago Bears, 17–13, with Emmitt running for 105 yards. Then in the divisional playoff game, Dallas fell apart. Detroit clobbered the Cowboys, 38–6, ending the Dallas season. But the Cowboys seemed on the brink of once again becoming one of the better teams in the league.

Although there were no fancy dances when Emmitt scored a touchdown, he did begin his own tradition: taking the scoring ball to his sports memorabilia store in Pensacola.

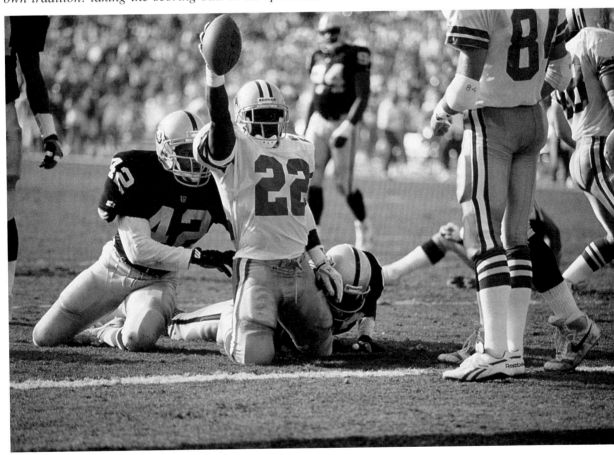

Among other things, Emmitt had become the youngest player in league history (at age 22 years, 7 months) to gain more than 1,500 yards in a season. He was named a starter in the postseason Pro Bowl game and, along with Buffalo's Thurman Thomas and Detroit's Barry Sanders, was considered one of the three best running backs in the league.

Before the outset of the 1992 season, Emmitt set his goal a bit higher. He usually aimed at 1,500 yards. Now he was aiming at 2,000.

He knew he was a major part of the Cowboys' attack. But one time during his rookie year he felt he wasn't getting enough carries. "The coaches would say in the meetings that we had to gain 100 yards on the ground," Emmitt recalled. "But how were we going to do it if I was only getting the ball 12 or 14 times a game? I felt we had to run to take the pressure off Troy [Aikman]. So I asked them to just give me the ball."

It was the only time Emmitt had complained. Now he knew he would get the football 20 or more times a game, and that's the way he liked it. The first game of the 1992 season was a perfect example. Emmitt carried the ball 27 times against archrival Washington, gaining 140 yards as the Cowboys opened their season with a big, 23–10, victory.

He continued to play at an All-Pro level, and Dallas kept winning. Other big games included 152 yards against the Raiders, 163 yards in a win over Philadelphia, and 174 yards versus Atlanta. In fact, in each of

It didn't take long for Emmitt to hit his stride in the NFL. His low center of gravity and slashing style can be seen in this game against the Philadelphia Eagles.

the seven games in which Emmitt gained more than 100 yards, the Cowboys won. More and more people marveled at his compact running style. He still wasn't flashy, but he was so hard to stop.

"He'll go into a pile and come out the other end," said Joe Brodsky. "He also has the ability to keep his legs clean—he very seldom gets hit with his feet on the ground. That's where you see people get hurt."

Emmitt himself almost made fun of his lack of blazing speed. "I run in slow motion," he said, "waiting to see what develops. But I'm constantly moving, low to the ground, trying to stay north and south."

He meant that he always tried to run upfield, not side to side like some runners. It was his strength and his instinct to run to the right spot that made him so good. And he was durable. In three years he hadn't missed a game or a start. He was always ready to carry a heavy load.

The Cowboys finished the 1992 season with a 13–3 record. They won the National Football Conference Eastern Division title. Only the San Francisco 49ers, with a 14–2 mark, had a better record than Dallas. And Emmitt Smith had produced his greatest season ever.

He led the NFL in rushing for the second straight year. This time he gained an amazing 1,713 yards on 373 carries, good for a career best 4.6 per carry average. He also grabbed 59 passes for another 335 yards. In addition, he set a Dallas record by running for 18 touchdowns. Not surprisingly, he was a consensus All-Pro choice and named a starter in the Pro Bowl for the second straight year. Now he and his teammates set their sights on the playoffs and—beyond that, if things went well—the Super Bowl.

SUPER BOWL FOR A SUPER GUY

In the first round of the 1992 play-offs, the Dallas Cowboys defeated the Philadelphia Eagles, 34–10. Emmitt ran for 114 yards on 25 carries as the team moved on to the NFC title game against the San Francisco 49ers.

This was a tough one. The Niners had a 7–3 lead after one period. But Emmitt scored from the 5-yard line in the second quarter to put his team back on top. By halftime, the two teams were tied at 10–10. At the end of three periods Dallas had a 17–13 lead. Then, early in the final quarter, the Cowboys drove again. From

In the NFC title game against San Francisco in January 1993, Emmitt ran for 114 yards. He caught seven passes for another 59 yards. The Cowboys won the game, 30–20, and were on their way to the Super Bowl.

the 16-yard line, Aikman hit Emmitt with a short pass, and the elusive running back took it into the end zone for another score. The kick made it 24–13.

When the game ended, Dallas had a 30–20 victory. Aikman completed 24 of 34 passes for 322 yards, while Emmitt gained 114 yards for the second straight game. He also caught seven passes for another 59 yards. Now the team was going to Super Bowl XXVII.

On January 31, 1993, the Cowboys met the Buffalo Bills at the Rose Bowl in Pasadena, California. Although the Bills had lost two straight Super Bowls, many people thought they would win this one. But the Cowboys played a great game from start to finish. After trailing 7–0 early, they just exploded on both offense and defense. The final score was 52–17. The Cowboys were Super Bowl champions.

In the Super Bowl blowout of Buffalo, Emmitt ran for 108 yards. He followed his blockers through the tough Bills defense.

A Super Bowl ring is an NFL player's most prized possession.

Emmitt closed the season with another strong game. This time he gained 108 yards on 22 carries to help his team to the title. He had been over 100 yards in all three playoff games, once again playing very well in the team's biggest games.

During the off-season, Emmitt still lived with his parents and continued to work toward his college degree. In the spring of 1993 he was just one semester short of graduation. He also had a store in Pensacola called Emmitt's 1st and 10 Trading Cards & Collectibles. The store was run by Emmitt's mother and his sister Marsha.

After three outstanding years, Emmitt's first contract with the Cowboys was up. He felt that the new pact should be a four-year one worth more than $3 million a year. It would be similar to the contract that Thurman Thomas had signed with Buffalo. Thomas was another superstar running back. Cowboys owner Jerry Jones offered Emmitt a deal that would pay him $2.4 million a year. Emmitt said no. "I was underpaid the first three years," he said. "Now it's time for me to be paid what I'm worth."

When 1993 training camp opened, Emmitt wasn't there. He was still holding out when the preseason games began. In fact, Emmitt said he would sit out the whole season if a new agreement couldn't be reached. He showed that he was true to his word when he sat out the first two games of the regular season. The Cowboys lost both games.

That's when owner Jones decided he had to sign his star runner. Emmitt finally signed a four-year, $13.6 million contract. He had what he wanted. He had become the highest-paid running back in the league at that time. And once he was back, the Cowboys began winning.

Seeing him running once again through NFL defenses, one of his teammates said, "We know we're not the Dallas Cowboys without Emmitt."

After Smith's holdout at the beginning of the 1993 season, Cowboy fans were relieved and happy to see Emmitt back on the sidelines with Coach Jimmy Johnson.

It was in his fifth game back that he ran for his team record of 237 yards, against Philadelphia. And a week later he shredded the tough New York Giants defense for 117 yards on 24 carries. It was the team's sixth straight win since his return, and Emmitt was once again among the top rushers in the league.

In game 12 he had another big day against the Eagles, gaining 172 yards as Dallas won, 23–17. Finally, with one game left in the regular season, the Cowboys had an 11–4 record and were meeting the Giants in a game that would decide the NFC's Eastern Division winner. In addition, Emmitt was in striking distance of his third straight NFL rushing title.

This was the game where Emmitt really put his stamp on greatness. His powerful running led to a 13–0 Dallas lead at halftime. Late in the second quarter he broke loose for a 46-yard gain. But when he was finally tackled by the Giants' Greg Jackson, he suffered a separated right shoulder. At the end of the half he had gained 109 yards on 19 carries. But the question now was would he be able to play in the second half?

There was no doubt that Emmitt was in severe pain, but he insisted on playing. "I talked to Emmitt two or three times throughout the second half," Coach Johnson said. "He kept telling me, 'I want to finish the ball game. I want to be the guy.' "

So Emmitt kept carrying the football. Every time he was tackled, his face showed the pain. But he wouldn't come out. Then the Giants rallied and tied the game at 13–13 at the end of regulation. It went into overtime.

Despite the constant pain, Emmitt began carrying the ball the first time the Cowboys got it. The team drove downfield. During the drive, Emmitt carried five more times for 16 tough yards and caught three Troy

Emmitt gained 168 yards against the Giants in the final game of the 1993 season despite severe pain from a shoulder injury. When the regular season ended, he was named the NFL's Most Valuable Player.

Aikman passes for another 24 yards. Finally, Eddie Murray booted a 41-yard field goal and the Cowboys had won it, 16–13.

Emmitt wound up with 168 yards on 32 carries. He also caught 10 passes for another 61 yards. That meant he had 229 of the Cowboys' 339 total yards. It was an amazing performance.

"My heart is as big as the world, and I wanted this game very badly," Emmitt said. "I wanted the team to have a week off."

The Cowboys were NFC East champs again and would have a bye (meaning they didn't have to play a game) in the first round of the play-offs. Emmitt's big day gave him 1,486 yards for the season and a third straight rushing title. He carried 283 times for a league best 5.3 per carry average. And he did it despite missing two full games, part of another with an injury, and just playing part-time in his first game back.

Now everyone knew just how good Emmitt Smith was. After the season ended he became the first Dallas Cowboy ever to be named the NFL's Most Valuable Player. And a short time later he received a second honor. He was voted the NFL's Player of the Year.

"The awards are a real honor," Emmitt said, "because they mean you've done what you're supposed to do and you've done it as well as anyone."

And in 1993, Emmitt Smith had done it better than anyone.

SUPER BOWL MVP

Now it was on to the playoffs. After a week off, the Cowboys had to play the tough Green Bay Packers. Emmitt admitted that his shoulder still wasn't 100 percent. But he said he would play, and he would not take any painkillers.

After a bruising first quarter, Green Bay took a 3–0 lead. But in the second, quarterback Aikman threw two touchdown passes and Eddie Murray kicked a 41-yard field goal. That made it 17–3 at the half. From there, the Cowboys went on to win, 27–17. Emmitt gained just 60 yards on 13 carries. It was obvious that his shoulder still wasn't right.

It would have to be better the next week. Now the Cowboys had to play the San Francisco 49ers for the NFC title. The winner would go on to the Super Bowl. A week earlier, the 49ers had blown out the New York Giants, 44–3.

But Dallas was ready. In the first quarter, Emmitt scored on a 5-yard run after catching a 28-yard pass from Aikman earlier in the drive. After the 49ers tied the game at 7–7 at the beginning of the second period, the Cowboys exploded. They scored three times to take a 28–7 lead at the half. Emmitt was a key figure in each drive, catching passes and making key runs.

In the second half, the Cowboys just played it out, winning easily, 38–21. They would be heading to the Super Bowl for a second straight year. As for Emmitt, he looked fine. He gained 88 yards on 23 carries and caught seven passes for another 85 yards.

"I feel like I can beat any linebacker one-on-one," Emmitt said, talking about his seven catches. "Several times the linebackers got over to me late. It was easier than I expected."

But would the Super Bowl be easy? Dallas would once again be playing the Buffalo Bills. Buffalo had now lost three straight Super Bowls, and they didn't want to lose a fourth. The game was played on January 30, 1994, at the new Georgia Dome in Atlanta.

In the first half, the Cowboys didn't look sharp. Buffalo was moving the ball with short passes and playing solid defense. When the Bills took a 13–6 lead into the locker room at halftime, fans wondered if the Cowboys would find the magic. But with the 1993 Cowboys, the magic often meant Emmitt Smith.

Buffalo took the second-half kickoff and were at their own 43-yard line when Thurman Thomas took a handoff and ran up the middle. But Thomas fumbled after a Leon Lett hit, and the ball squirted loose. Safety James Washington picked the fumble up and took off on a 46-yard broken-field return for a touchdown. The kick tied the game at 13–13.

Then the next time the Cowboys got the ball, Emmitt took over. Dallas started at its own 36-yard line. Quarterback Aikman just gave the ball to Emmitt and let him loose. Using the same running style he always had, Emmitt ripped off one gain after another. He carried the ball five straight times, then twice more. His final carry was a neat 15-yard touchdown run that gave his team the lead.

Dallas had driven 64 yards in eight plays. Emmitt carried the ball on seven of those plays and gained 61 of the yards. The conversion made it 20–13, and the Cowboys were on their way. Then early in the fourth quarter Emmitt scored again, this time from the 1-yard line on a clutch, fourth-down carry. From there, the Cowboys went on to win, 30–13. They were Super Bowl champs for the second straight year.

In the 1994 Super Bowl, the Cowboys beat the Bills, 30–13, with Emmitt gaining 132 yards. Here he eludes Buffalo's Jeff Wright on his way to a 15-yard touchdown. Emmitt was later named the game's MVP to cap a sensational year.

As for Emmitt Smith, he had carried the ball 30 times for 132 yards and was named the game's Most Valuable Player.

"We came back to this game with a mission," Emmitt said afterward. "It was a super year for me and a super year for my teammates."

Emmitt has continued to have long-range goals. He has talked of gaining more than 2,000 yards in the regular season. And he has mentioned topping Walter Payton's all-time rushing record of more than 16,000 yards. He has also purchased property in Pensacola, where he intends to build a house. Not surprisingly, he has planned the house to be big enough for every member of his family who wants to live there.

As his high school coach, Dwight Thomas, once said, "The Smiths should be the role model for all American families."

Now Emmitt has become one of the biggest stars in all sports. He has been an important part of football's best team, a team that could win even more Super Bowls in the later 1990s. Yet he has remained hardworking and humble. Shortly after the team's second Super Bowl win over Buffalo, Emmitt was asked about his goals. He kept it very simple:

"I want to become a better football player and a better person," Emmitt Smith said.

Football has always taken second place to family for Emmitt Smith. Here members of the Smith family pose with him at his store in Pensacola.

EMMITT SMITH: HIGHLIGHTS

1969   Born on May 15 in Pensacola, Florida.

1983   Enters Escambia High School. Gains 1,525 yards rushing.

1984   Gains 2,424 yards rushing in 14 games as Escambia wins the Florida state championship.

1985   Gains 2,914 yards rushing in 14 games as Escambia again wins the state championship.

1986   Gains 1,937 yards rushing in only 11 games.
            Named High School All-American.
            Named National Player of the Year by several organizations.

1987   Enters University of Florida.
            Gains 1,341 yards rushing.
            Named Freshman Player of the Year by United Press International and *Sporting News*.

1988   Gains 988 yards rushing in sophomore year despite missing two games.
            Named to the All-Southeastern Conference first team.

1989   Gains 1,599 yards rushing and 207 yards on receptions.
            Finishes college career having set 58 school records in only three seasons.
            Named All-American.

1990   Joins the Dallas Cowboys of the National Football League (NFL).
            Gains 937 yards rushing, the best total among NFL rookie running backs.
            Named to the All-Rookie team.
            Named NFL Offensive Rookie of the Year by the Associated Press.

1991   Leads the NFL with 1,563 yards rushing.
            Named All-Pro.

1992   Leads the NFL with 1,713 yards rushing.
            Named All-Pro.

1993   Dallas wins Super Bowl XXVII in January.
            Leads the NFL with 1,486 yards rushing in the regular season.
            Wins the Most Valuable Player (MVP) Award for the regular season and is named All-Pro.

1994   Named Super Bowl MVP after leading the Dallas Cowboys to victory in Super Bowl XXVIII.

FIND OUT MORE

Duden, Jane and Susan Osberg. *Football*. New York: Macmillan, 1991.

Gutman, Bill. *Football*. North Bellmore, New York: Marshall Cavendish, 1990.

Marx, Doug. *Running Backs*. Vero Beach, Florida.: Rourke Corp., 1992.

Sullivan, George. *All About Football*. New York: Putnam Publishing Group, 1990.

How to write to
Emmitt Smith:

Emmitt Smith
c/o The Dallas Cowboys
Cowboys Center
One Cowboys Parkway
Dallas, Texas 75063

INDEX